You Taught Me Love

A special gift for:

Written by **MISTY BLACK**   Artwork by **MARINA BATRAK**

Berry Patch Press LLC

You Taught Me Love • With Love Collection
Copyright © 2020 Berry Patch Press

Edited by Amanda Mills & Shannon Jade
Book & Cover Design by Praise Saflor

Library of Congress Control Number:2019953515

ISBN Paperback 978-1-951292-07-2
ISBN Ebook 978-1-951292-08-9
ISBN Hardback 978-1-951292-09-6

First Edition 2020

 Berry Patch Press LLC
www.berrypatchpress.com

Watch for the companion coloring book, as well as other books in the *With Love* collection. *When You Feel Better* is the perfect book to take you on an adventure when you're too sick to get out of bed.

Other books by author Misty Black

Fizzle Fun Series:

Unicorns, Magic, and Slime, Oh My!
My Mom the Fairy

Punk and Friends Series:

Punk the Skunk Learns to Say Sorry
Quilliam Learns to Control His Temper

With Love Collection:

When You Feel Better: A Get Well Soon Gift

Find lesson plans, teacher help guides, free downloads, and promotions at berrypatchpress.com

mistyblackauthor@gmail.com

Not long ago, in a place very near,
A little one sat with her mother to hear
The three greatest words that can ever be said.
To learn what they are, let's continue ahead.

"I love you, Sweet Pea," Mama said to her child.
"And I love you too!" The girl winked as she smiled.
"How much?" teased her mom, sensing what was in store.
A new game began about who loved who more...

I love you as wide as my arms.

Your arms can stretch far,
But just as you are,
I love you a lot more than that.

I love you as soft as Koala.

He's cuddly and fluffy,
But it's not a toughie.
I love you a lot more than that.

I love you as fast as my frog.

He's jumping up quick,
But it isn't a trick
That I love you a lot more than that.

I love you as long as my hair!

Your hair's grown so much,
And it's soft to the touch,
But I love you a lot more than that.

I love you as tall as the roof.

The roof's really tall.
Let's be sure not to fall.
And I love you a lot more than that.

I love you as yummy as berries.

They're juicy and sweet.
Thanks for sharing this treat.
Still, I love you a lot more than that.

I love you as happy as splashing.

Come closer, let's dance.
But it isn't by chance
That I love you a lot more than that.

I love you as bright as a rainbow.

Its colorful light
Is a beautiful sight.
But I love you a lot more than that.

I love you as hot as the sun.

The sunshine is warm.
It has cast out the storm.
Still, I love you a lot more than that.

I love you as pretty as flowers.

They're beautiful, dear. They bring joy every year.
And I love you a lot more than that.

I love you as high as the hills.

We're certainly high,
Almost touching the sky.
But I love you a lot more than that.

I love you as big as the world.

It's wonderfully grand.
But please understand
That I love you a lot more than that.

I love you as open as space...and beyond!

Is that really true?
That's how much I love you!
Who taught you to love me so much?

I learned it from you.
Through all that you do,
You taught me to love oh-so much.

The three greatest words that have ever been said
Are very contagious and like to be spread.
So tell someone special "I love you" today.
I think you should try it and see what they say.

**When they ask you how much, do you know what to do?
The power to show and share love lies in you.**

Dedication

Dedicated to my spunky little Sweet Pea.
I love you as warm as the sun. Thank you for lighting up my life.
Also dedicated to my mother. I love you as bright as a rainbow. You
filled my soul with color. —Misty Black

Dedicated to my mother. She, like no one else,
knows how much soul, work, and love is invested in these illustrations.
I sincerely wish that all readers of this book really learn to appreciate,
love, and protect their mothers, and also to take care of their little
daughters with love. Thank you to author Misty Black for a great idea
and a sweet story. —Marina Batrak

Did you know...

There's a hidden ladybug and at
least one hidden heart on every spread!
Read the story again and see if you can find them all.

Koala, from *When You Feel Better*, is part of the story.
And we have a new friend, Frog. Look for them in every
adventure.

About the Author

Misty Black enjoys picture books as much as her children do, if not more! Why? Because a good book can take you anywhere in the world!

Misty enjoys thinking of new ways picture books can be enjoyed. She writes books that can be given as presents, like greeting cards or flowers, and she writes about topics that translate to both children and adults. She is the author of several children's books, including *When You Feel Better; Unicorns, Magic, and Slime, Oh My;* and *Punk the Skunk Learns to Say Sorry.* You can email her at mistyblackauthor@gmail.com.

Follow Misty at 🇫 📷 📌 Misty Black Author.

To sign up for promos and new releases,
visit berrypatchpress.com

Thank you for your purchase. If you're able to show your support by leaving an honest review, it would be very appreciated.

About the Illustrator

Marina Batrak

Art, painting, and creativity are Marina's life. She has loved drawing since the moment she learned how to hold a pencil. She loves taking photographs, playing piano, scrapbooking, and arranging flowers. She also illustrated *When You Feel Better: A Get Well Soon Gift.*

Follow Marina at marina_batrak

Made in the USA
Middletown, DE
11 February 2020